# POSTAL SERVICE

James Nixon

W
FRANKLIN WATTS
LONDON•SYDNEY

First published in 2009 by
Franklin Watts
338 Euston Road
London NW1 3BH

Franklin Watts Australia
Level 17/207 Kent Street
Sydney NSW 2000



ISBN: 978 0 7496 8407 5

Dewey classification number: 383





A CIP catalogue record for this book is available from the British Library.

Planning and production by Discovery Books Limited
Editor: James Nixon
Designer: Ian Winton
Commissioned photography: Bobby Humphrey

Photographs: Alamy: p. 21 bottom (Jack Sullivan); The British Postal Museum & Archive: pp. 19, 20 bottom, 27; Discovery Picture Library: pp. 7 top, 10, 12, 21 top, 23 top, 25 middle (Chris Fairclough); DHL International Ltd.: p. 23 bottom; Getty Images: pp. 6 top (Peter Cade), 20 top (Peter Macdiarmid); Istockphoto.com: p. 8 bottom (Jonathan Maddock).

Cover photos: Bobby Humphrey: bottom; Discovery Picture Library: top, bottom right (Chris Fairclough); Shutterstock: title background (Szabo Photography).

The author, packager and publisher would like to thank the Royal Mail and Worcester Mail Centre for their help and participation in this book.

Printed in China

Franklin Watts is a division of Hachette Children's Books, an Hachette UK company.
www.hachette.co.uk

# Contents

You've got mail 6
Writing an address 8
Sending mail 10
Collection time 12
At the mail centre 14
Marking the post 16
Sorting it out 18
Mail on the move 20
Parcel post 22
Ready for the rounds 24
To the door 26
Glossary 28
Further information 29
Index 30

**Words in bold are in the glossary on page 28.**

# You've got mail

**Do you like receiving letters and parcels in the post? Have you ever posted a letter to a friend or sent a postcard when you are on holiday? Nearly every morning mail gets delivered through your letterbox.**

The packages that come to your door can be big or small. There may be a birthday present or a birthday card.

There might be an item that you have ordered from the **Internet**. There may be something less exciting, like a telephone bill.

## A postal network

The postal service is a great way for people to transport things to each other and keep in touch. It doesn't matter how far you live from someone, you can always use the post. Mail can be sent to anywhere in the world.

But how does the postal service work? When we post a letter how can we be sure it will get to exactly the right place?

**Royal Mail**
The company in charge of sending post across the UK is Royal Mail. They deliver around 84 million letters and parcels every day!

# Writing an address

**When you are sending a friend a birthday card in the post, what must you do? First you need to write your friend's name and address on the envelope clearly.**

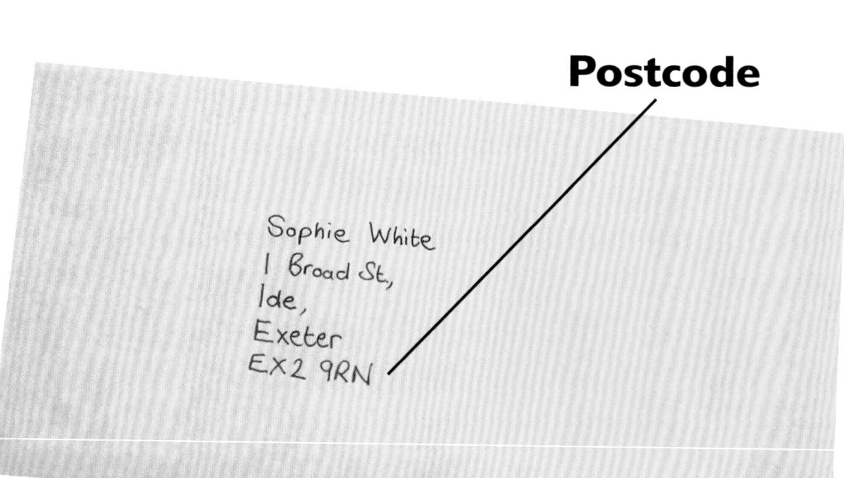

Don't forget to add the **postcode** below the address. This is the most important bit. It helps pinpoint exactly where the mail needs to go. Without it your letter might take longer to be delivered or could even go missing.

Now stick the correct stamp in the top right-hand corner (above) and it is ready to put in a postbox (right).

## Code cracking

Everyone's postcode has four parts, which are a step-by-step guide to where the mail is going.

The first one or two letters stand for the area. EX stands for Exeter.

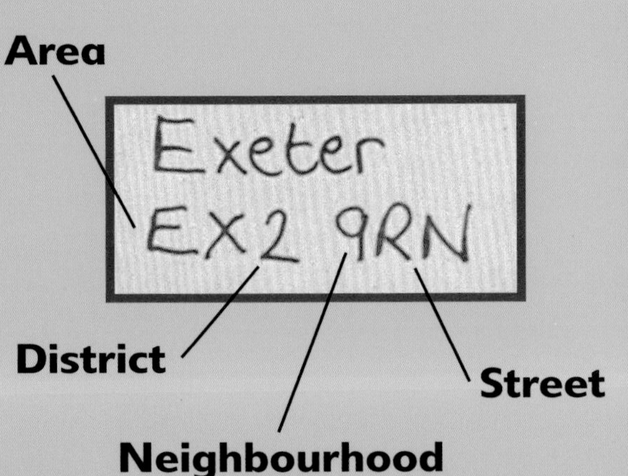


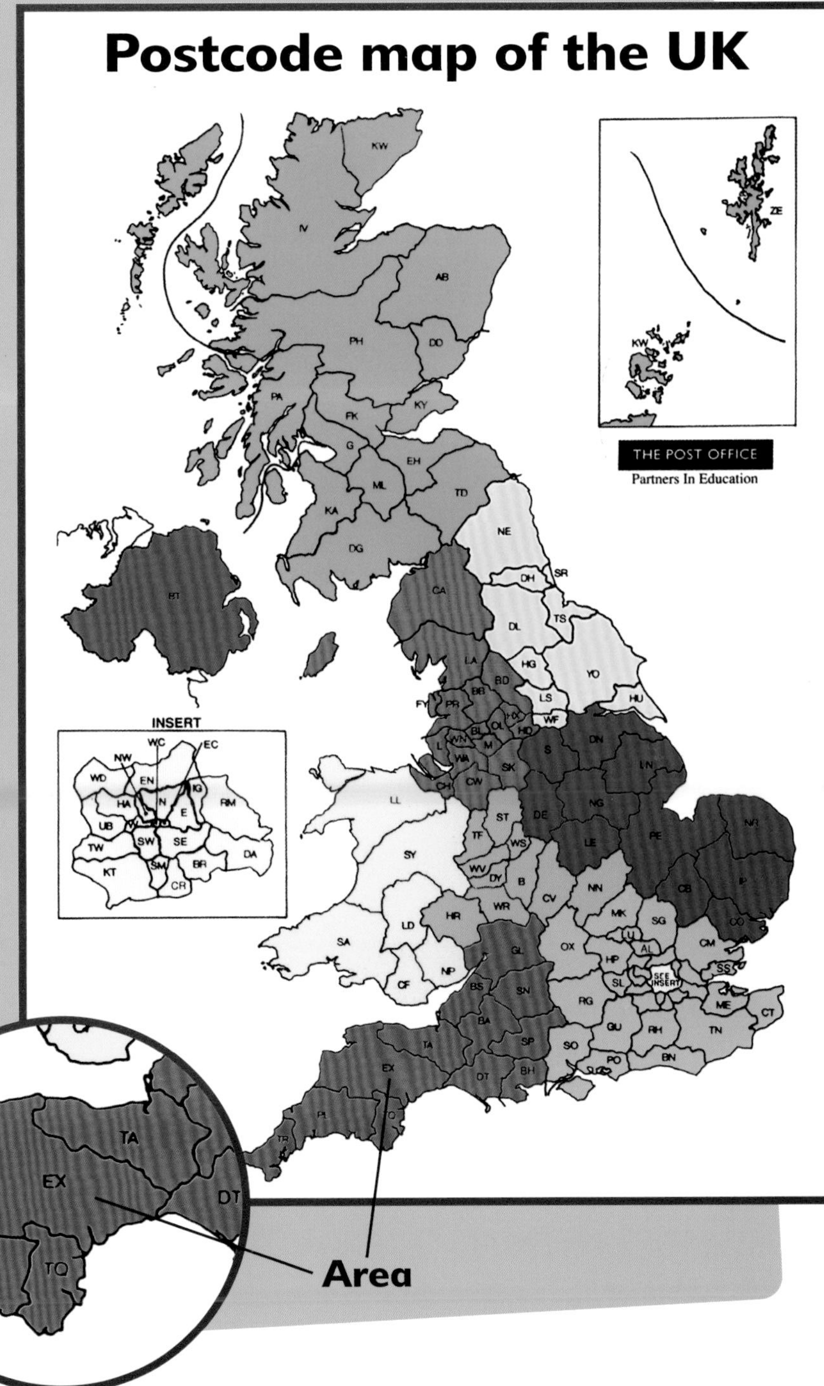


Each area is divided into **districts**, which are each given a number, like 2. The third part, which is usually one number, stands for the neighbourhood in the district. The final part tells the postal service which street the letter needs to go to.

# Sending mail

**You can choose a first-class or second-class stamp for your letter. First-class stamps are more expensive, but get your letter sent quicker.**

## Posting parcels

If you are posting something larger or heavier than a normal letter, you will probably have to pay extra.

Take larger packages to your local **post office** and they will measure it, weigh it and stamp it for you.

## Stamp it!

The stamp on a letter shows that the postage has been paid for. The idea of using postage stamps began in the UK in 1840. Now stamps are used all over the world. Look at these stamps. Can you work out which country each stamp comes from?

## Special deliveries

If your package is very important you might choose to send it by special or recorded delivery. You can do this at the post office. A special delivery is the best way to get your package to its destination quickly. A recorded delivery has to be signed for by your friend when he or she receives it. This makes sure your package doesn't get sent to the wrong place.

# Collection time

**At certain times each day a postal worker comes to collect the mail from the postbox. When you next post a letter, look at the time marked on the front of the box. This tells you when your letter will be collected.**

## My name is Gurmail

I open each postbox in my area with a different key and load the letters into the back of my van. I also collect sacks of mail that has been posted at the post office. Once all the mail has been collected I take it to the mail centre to be sorted.

# Postboxes

Postboxes can be found all over the country. They come in all different shapes and sizes. The big letters on the front of the box tell you who was king or queen when the box was put there.

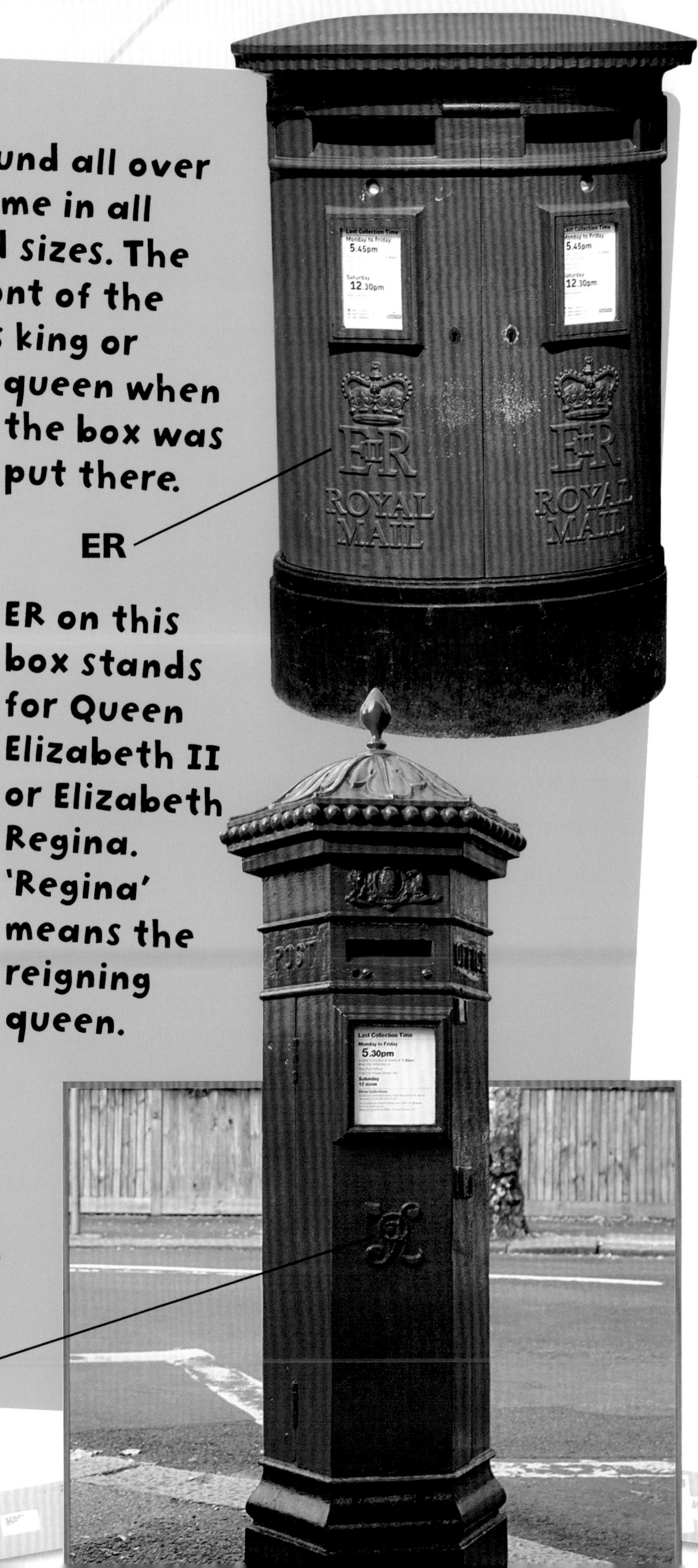


ER

ER on this box stands for Queen Elizabeth II or Elizabeth Regina. 'Regina' means the reigning queen.

GR

What do you think GR and VR stand for? (The answer is on page 29.)

VR

# At the mail centre

**The van arrives at the mail centre with the post ready to be sorted.**

The sacks of mail are unloaded onto trolleys and wheeled into the sorting office.

## Sorting by size

The first job is to separate the bigger items from the smaller sized letters as they are sorted in different places in the mail centre. The mailbags are emptied onto a **conveyor belt**, which carries the letters into a big drum (right). Inside the drum the letters are tumbled to sort them into different sizes.

**My name is Emma**

I work in the mail centre. I keep an eye on the automatic sorting process and make sure the machinery is working properly. The machines often get jammed up. In this job you have to be able to stand on your feet for long periods. A lot of the time I am carrying sacks of mail and pushing trolleys around the centre.

# Marking the post

**The letter you posted then travels along to the automatic letter facer.**

Here your letter passes through a **sensor** (right) that checks which way the letter is facing.

It is then turned the correct way up as it moves through a series of belts (below).

A **postmark** is then printed across the stamp in the top right corner. That is why you must stick the stamp there! The postmark stops anybody from reusing the stamp.

# Reading the postcode

Next the **Integrated Mail Processor** (IMP) sorts the mail by reading the postcodes. If the IMP can read the postcode it prints a pink bar code across the package. The pattern of pink dots printed depends on the postcode. Now you know why the postcode is so important.

27.08.08 Worcester 05:42 pm 13500185

**Postmark**

Sophie White
1 Broad St,
Ide,
Exeter
EX2 9RN

**Pink bar code**

▲ **Each letter goes on a journey through the IMP machinery where it is marked and sorted.**

The IMP has to deal with hundreds of thousands of letters each day. It is constantly being fed with newly arrived mail and will go on working throughout the night.

# Sorting it out

**Once your letter has a pink bar code printed on it, it can finally be sorted into the area that it needs to be delivered to.**

The last part of the IMP is an electronic sorting machine. It reads the pink marks and sorts all the letters with similar marks into the same pigeon hole.

This enormous bank of pigeon holes is the end of the line for the automatically sorted mail.

## Hand sorting

Letters that have no postcode, or cannot be read by the IMP are removed to be sorted by hand, but this is much slower.

### Night trains

Before mechanical sorting was introduced, all of the post was sorted by hand into racks. To save time, mail was sorted during the night in railway carriages as it travelled to its destination. In 2004 sorting mail on the train came to an end.

# Mail on the move

**Now your letter is ready to be sent to the part of the country where it will be delivered. The letters in each pigeon hole are bagged up and taken away by a van or lorry to another smaller sorting office near their destination.**

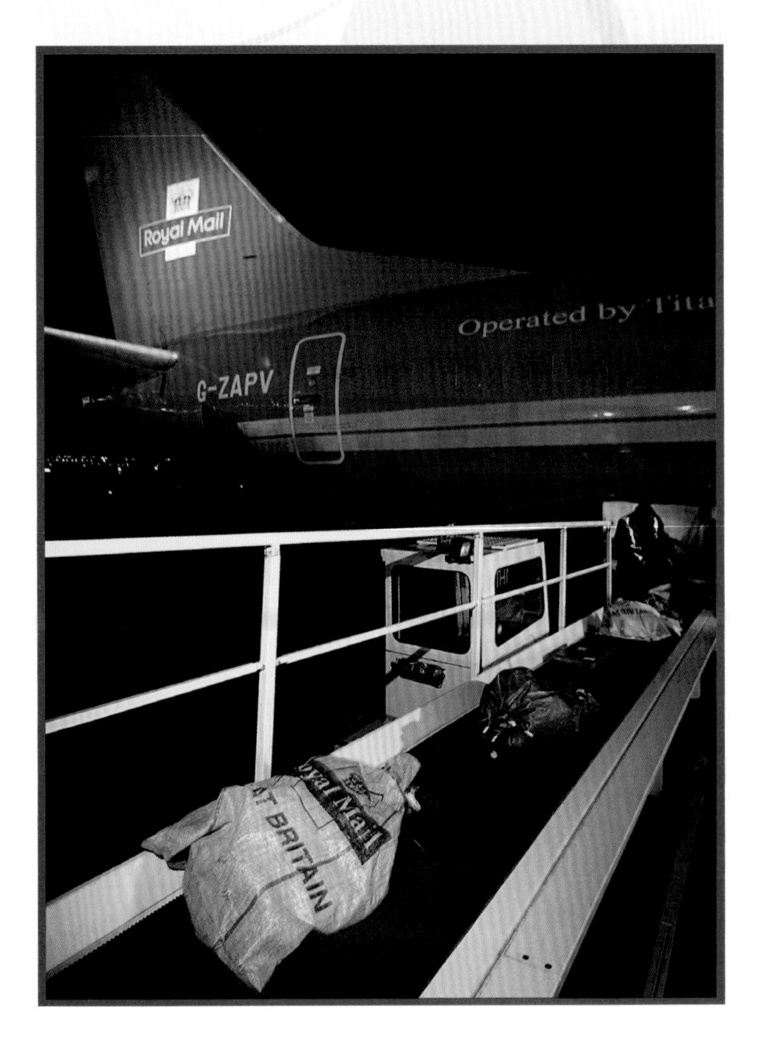


## Trains and planes

Mailbags that have a long way to go are taken by train (below) or plane.

Mail is often carried in ordinary passenger planes, but the Royal Mail also have their own aircraft (above).

# International mail

If you are sending a letter abroad it will usually go by plane. As well as a stamp you should attach an **air mail label**. Sending mail to another country can be expensive. To make it as cheap as possible use lightweight paper and these special lightweight envelopes. If you are sending a larger package it is cheaper to send it across the sea by ship. This is called **surface mail**. It will take much longer though. A package going to Australia could take 12 weeks to get there!

# Parcel post

**What happens to the packages at the mail centre that can't be sorted by the IMP?**

Parcels are taken to another part of the centre where they are sorted by hand. Postal workers do all the jobs that the machines do for letters.

## Mark and sort

They cancel the stamp by printing a postmark (left), and sort the packages into the areas that they are going (above). The sacks are each marked with a different postcode.

## Parcel Force

Bigger packages are not delivered to your door by the postal worker who delivers your letters. A separate part of the postal service called Parcel Force carries these items around the country.

## Couriers

Not all packages are carried by the Royal Mail. Couriers are companies that offer special services, such as next-day delivery to Europe. However, they are generally more expensive than the usual postal service and are mainly used by businesses.

# Ready for the rounds

**After the mail has been sorted and transported overnight it arrives at the local sorting office very early the next morning. Here the letters are sorted again into smaller areas and districts.**

## Early start

The postal workers that deliver your mail start work long before you wake up. They come into the local office and pick up the post for their own **rounds**. Before they set off they sort their pile of post into the order they are going to deliver it. A **frame** (above) helps postal workers do this. Now they are ready to go.

# Doing the rounds

Different postal workers use different vehicles to do their rounds.

If the addresses are close to the sorting office they can walk around the whole route from door to door, or use a bicycle (above right). If the rounds are far away a van or other motor vehicle is needed.

▶ **On their rounds postal workers use boxes like this one to store post. This saves them carrying it all at once.**

# To the door

**Your letter is finally ready to finish its journey. Think back to how far your letter has come.**

It has been stamped, sorted and transported with millions of other letters. Yet it is still delivered to the right address by the next morning. The postal worker delivers all of the post through the letterbox including your letter.

If the postal worker has an item sent by recorded delivery, he or she will knock on the door and ask for a signature. When the morning's rounds are finished the postal worker goes back to the postboxes to collect the day's newly posted mail.

## Town and country

Postal workers in towns and cities don't have to travel very far because the houses are so close together. But in the country they may have to travel a huge area just to deliver to a few houses. This postal worker is using a **quad bike** to get from house to house on this **remote** Scottish island.

# Glossary

**Air mail** Post that travels by air.

**Automatic letter facer** The part of the IMP that turns letters around to face the right way up.

**Conveyor belt** A moving band of material used for transporting objects from one place to another.

**Destination** The place where a letter is being sent to.

**Districts** Small regions that make up a county.

**Frame** The rack that postal workers use to sort the post before delivery.

**Integrated Mail Processor (IMP)** A huge machine in the mail centre that each letter travels through to be marked and sorted.

**Internet** The worldwide computer network that allows information, such as a shopping order, to be exchanged from one computer to another.

**Post office** A place that sells stamps and deals with letters and parcels.

**Postcode** The letters and numbers at the end of an address that help the sorting of mail.

**Postmark** The mark stamped on a letter to show that the stamp has been used. It also tells you the date, time and place that the letter was sorted.

**Quad bike** A motorcycle with four large tyres.

**Remote** Describes a place located far away from a town or city.

**Rounds** A job that involves visiting a number of houses in turn.

**Sensor** A device used to detect something.

**Surface mail** Post that is sent by land and sea.

# Further information

## Books

*Postman (When I'm at Work)*, Sue Barraclough, 2006 (Franklin Watts)

*The Post Office (Out and About)*, Sue Barraclough, 2006 (Franklin Watts)

*A Letter to New Zealand*, Alison Howes, 2005 (Collins)

## Websites

**www.bbc.co.uk/dna/h2g2/A1082558**

This site gives you a short history of the postal service.

**http://postalheritage.org.uk**

This is the online website for the British Postal Museum.

**www.junior-philatelists.com**

With the help of this website you can find out all about stamps and start a collection.

**Note to parents and teachers:** Every effort has been made by the Publishers to ensure that these websites are suitable for children, that they are of the highest educational value, and that they contain no inappropriate or offensive material. However, because of the nature of the Internet, it is impossible to guarantee that the contents of these sites will not be altered. We strongly advise that Internet access is supervised by a responsible adult.

Answer to the question on page 13: GR stands for George Rex (George VI was the king between 1936–52). VR stands for Victoria Regina (Victoria was the queen between 1837–1901).

# Index


addresses 8, 25, 26
air mail 20, 21
automatic letter facer 16

couriers 23

frames 24

Integrated Mail Processor 17, 18, 19, 22

mail centres 12, 14, 15

Parcel Force 23
parcels 6, 10, 22, 23
post office 10, 11, 12, 28
postal workers 12, 15, 22, 23, 24, 25, 26, 27
postboxes 8, 12, 13, 26
postcodes 8, 9, 17, 22
postmarks 16, 22

recorded deliveries 11, 26
rounds 24, 25
Royal Mail 7, 20, 23

sorting mail 15, 17, 18, 19, 22
sorting offices 14, 20, 24
special deliveries 11
stamps 8, 10, 11, 16
surface mail 21

trains 19, 20

vans 12, 14, 20, 25